The Official

TEXT MSG HANDBOOK

VOL.1

A FULL-FLEDGED GUIDE TO

TEXT MESSAGE COMMUNICATION

Justin Bilancieri

Written by Justin Bilancieri

Edited by Joanna Bilancieri

Copyright © 2016 Justin Bilancieri
All rights reserved.

ISBN: 1540648680
ISBN-13: 978-1540648686

Thank you, Earth,
and everything you
provide.

This guidebook will help you understand and more effectively communicate via text messaging.

These pages explain the etiquette, grammar, and shorthand behind this relatively new form of communication.

You will walk away feeling refreshed and thrilled with your newly found skills. This will pretty much make all your days from here on out a lot better.

Your friends will thank you. Your children, grandchildren, and great-grandchildren will thank you. Your co-workers and clients will thank you. You will thank you.

Thank you.

TOC

Etiquette...................................1
Grammar................................5
Shorthand..........................9
Conclusion........................55
Notes................................57

Brevity is the soul of wit.

— William Shakespeare

Etiquette

Let's face it. Some people have it and some people don't. Some are courteous and others aren't. Well, that same courtesy also carries over into texting. For those who cherish etiquette, here are a few points to consider:

• Don't feel like a text is always the most important thing in the world. Jumping to see who's texting when your boyfriend, girlfriend, mom, dad, son, daughter, or whoever is talking with you, is saying to that person YOU ARE BORING.
[See note.]

[Note] This person might be boring, but this is a chapter on text messaging etiquette, not self-help facilitation.

• Polite interruptions to take important texts are completely acceptable. Kindly ask for the small amount of time it will take for you to handle your text. Assure your company that you look forward to hearing the rest of his/her story in just a minute.

• There is no need to feel obliged to respond to texts right away. Taking time to think about your responses is perfectly acceptable. This goes the other way around, too. If you don't get a response right away, it doesn't automatically mean that you're being blown off or that you're not important. In fact, some people even shut their phones off, believe it or not. Remember, there is no need to panic. [See note.]

[Note] Ever.

• Do realize that people lose/misplace their phones, make love, take showers, sleep, and sometimes just can't be interrupted. So, don't take it personally if they don't get back with you right away.

• Don't text again. Wait for the reply. If it's that important, texting again is acceptable, but only to ask if the text was received and for a reply ASAP. If still no reply, call. Yes, it's actually still okay to call someone. [See note.]

[Note] This doesn't apply to people you don't already know, like the girl who hesitatingly gave you her number on Friday night.

- Although replying to texts right away is not imperative, feel free to be like most C-suite execs and promptly reply (when not in another's company as earlier mentioned). It makes your text recipient feel important. It also makes way for the next exciting thing in your life to happen.

- Be spontaneous. This applies to all aspects of your life and it certainly goes for text messaging.

- Be succinct. Here is your chance to say a lot with a little. Less is more. Short texts allow us to spend more time actually communicating face-to-face. Yes, face-to-face communication still exist.

- Feel free to speak lovingly from your heart. Say meaningful things while you text. It will feel good. Again, this applies to all areas of your life.

- But, don't try and explain something heavy or deep to someone with a text. The emotion just is not there.

- Okay, some of you may not like this one, but texting and driving do not mix well. I repeat, texting and driving do not mix well. So just pull over or wait until you arrive at your destination to text.

Take a deep breath. In fact, take several. Inhale.... Exhale....

You are much cooler than you were 5 minutes ago. I mean, you were cool, but now that you're acquiring new texting skills, you're that much cooler. Seriously. So, keep turning these pages and let that new coolness set in. Feels good, doesn't it?

Grammar

The main point of texting is to keep communication simple, fast, and to the point. This allows for efficient use of your time and the recipient's time. It allows for direct communication. I know the latter can be difficult for some of you, but hang in there and you will love it in no time. Being a better texter will make you one happy human now and in the future.

So, as you text, remember this: GRAMMAR CAN GO RIGHT OUT THE DOOR...and that's okay!

Okay, wait. A couple things here...

1. If you are texting someone for the first time, proper grammar may be appropriate. In fact, there is nothing wrong with ever using proper grammar.

2. Remember, we have little time on this little planet. So, let's not waste a drop of it! If you can communicate to me in half the amount of time it takes to communicate it to me with good grammar, then GREAT! Go for it!

With that said, if you still prefer to write out complete and eloquent sentences, okay at least complete sentences, that is perfectly acceptable. However, for most of us, texting is about clear, quick communication.

Below are some key points to consider when drafting up your next text:

Capitalization - no need for it. That little shift button is great, but really, we can do without it for the majority of our texting. [See note.]

[Note] When we get to the acronym section, there are exceptions to this rule.

Articles of Speech - don't always need 'em. I can write, "What a lovely day" or I can write "Lovely day". I can say, "They clearly missed the point" or I can say, "They clearly missed point". Sure, in each case the latter is not as eloquent, but it gets the point across quickly and that is the whole reason for texting.

Spelling - drop vowels and obvious consonants, and there u hv it. I can write about the lovly day and u stll get it. Plus, auto spelling will often correct it for you.

Spacing - leave it out when you can, but dontoverdoit. Although itcan befun, it can become hardtoread or evenannoying.

"ing" - drop the i and the g and there you have it. No need for apostrophes either. Examples: workn or wrkn, playn, and livn.

So a 21st century text may look something like this: thx 4bn thr 4 me! U mean wrlds 2 me! ilu xo

Ok, now that you have your grammar down let's talk about some shrt-hnd or txt msg syntax. This will make you a power texter and your life will get better and better and better.

First learn the meaning
of what you say, and
then speak.

- Epictetus

Keep in mind that text messaging is contextual. May this list in no way stunt your creativity. It's simply a guide to the most commonly used text abbreviations.

Shorthand (texting syntax)

- The Alphabet -

a - a

b - be or baby or boy or bee

c - see

d - definitely

e - e-mail or a party substance

f - funny or an angry curse

g - great

G - friend or mate as in What up, G?

h - hi or hey

i - I

j - joke

k - okay

l - love

m - mmm or correct or yep

n - no or "and"

o - oh or hug

O - Oh! or big hug
p - pm or phone or probably
q - question
Q - important question or are you serious?
r - are
s - silly, sly, or sexy
S - very silly, very sly, or very sexy
t - telephone
u - you
U - YOU!
v - very
w - with
W - whatever
x - kiss
X - big wet kiss
y - yes
Y - yes, absolutely
z - sleep or sleeping or sleep time

- Numbers & Symbols -

1 - one or won

2 - to, too, or two

4 - for, four, or as a prefix as in 4tune (fortune)

8 - used as a suffix as in l8 (late) or m8 (mate)

@ - at

? - question

:) - happy or smiling at you

:p - happy with my tongue out

:)) - very happy

:D - thrilled or laughing

:P - sticking my tongue out at you

;) - smiling wink

: O - Really?!

411 - information

911 - emergency

831 - I love you (8 letters, 3 words, 1 meaning)

? - question or I don't understand

<3 - love or friendship

<33 - lots of love
<333 - totally loving you

- 2 Character Syntax -

bw - between
dt - downtown
ez - easy
fr - from
jk - just kidding or joking
lk - like
lu - love you
lv - love
np - no problem

- 3 Character Syntax -

4ev - forever
aap - always a pleasure
abt - about
add - address
atb - all the best
btw - by the way

lol - laughing out loud
lvu - love you
omg - oh my God
wbu - What about you?

- 4 Character Syntax -

abt2 - about to
ttyl - talk to you later
ttys - talk to you soon
haha- laughing
hehe - mischievous giggling

- More Common Syntax -

.02 - my/your two cents worth
143 - I love you (first word 1 letter, second word 4 letters, third word 3 letters)
20 - what is your location
2ez - too easy
2g2bt - too good to be true
2m2h - too much to handle
2mi or tmi - too much information

tmrw - tomorrow

tnite - tonight

2nt - tonight

idk - I don't know

511 - too much Info

459 - I love you (ily is 459 using keypad numbers)

4col - for crying out loud

4eae - forever and ever

4nr - foreigner

^5 - high-five

555 - sobbing or crying

6y - sexy

86 - over

88 - bye-bye

999 - more power to you

Can you think of any more?

- A -

a3 - anytime, anywhere, anyplace
aaf - as a friend
aak - asleep at keyboard
aamof - as a matter of fact
aap - always a pleasure
aar - at any rate
abc - already been chewed
abt - about
acdnt - accident
adbb - all done, bye-bye
addy - address
adih - another day in heaven
adip - another day in paradise
admin - administrator
adn - any day now
afaiaa - as far as I am aware
afaic - as far as I am concerned
afaics - as far as I can see
afaik - as far as I know
afpoe - a fresh pair of eyes

ah - at home
aight - alright
aisb - as I said before
aitr - adult in the room
aka - also known as
alol - actually laughing out loud
alrt - alright
aml - all my love
amof - as a matter of fact
app - application
asig - and so it goes
asap - as soon as possible
atb - all the best
ateotd - at the end of the day
awsm - awesome
aydy - are you done yet?
ays - are you serious?
ayt - are you there?
aytmtb - and you're telling me this because..?
ayw - as you wish

- B -

b& - banned
b2w - back to work
b9 - boss is watching
b4 - before
b4n - bye for now
basor - breathing a sigh of relief
bau - business as usual
bay - back at ya
bb - be back
bbl - be back later
bbq - barbeque
bc - because
bco - big crush on
bcoy - big crush on you
bd - big deal
bday - birthday
bf - best friend(s)
bff - best friend(s) forever
b/f - boyfriend
bfflnmw - best friends for life, no matter what

bfd - big freaking deal
bg - background (personal info request)
bhl8 - be home late
bib - boss is back
bif - before I forget
bil - brother-in-law
bion - believe it or not
bk - be kind
bl - belly laugh
blnt - better luck next time
bm - bite me or bowel movement
bme - based on my experience
bn - bad news
bol - best of luck
bolo - be on the look out
booms - bored out of my skull
bosmkl - bending over smacking my knee laughing
bot - back on topic
bplm - big person little mind
brb - be right back
br - best regards

brd - bored
brh - be right here
brt - be right there
bsf - but seriously folks
bsts - better safe than sorry
bt - but or butt
bta - but then again
btdt - been there, done that
btt - back to topic
btw - by the way
btycl - booty call
by&m - between you and me
byob - bring your own beer or booze
byoc - bring your own computer

- C -

c&g - chuckle & grin
c4n - ciao for now
cb - coffee break or chat break
cd9 - code 9, meaning parents are around
cfs - care for secret?
cfy - calling for you

cid - consider it done
clab - crying like a baby
cm - call me
cmb - call me back
cmiiw - correct me if I'm wrong
cmon - come on
cnt - continued (in) next text
cob - close of business
cr8 - create
craft - can't remember a freakin' thing
crb - come right back
crz - crazy
csg - chuckle, snicker, grin
csl - can't stop laughing
ctc - care to chat?
cthu - cracking the heck up
ctn - can't talk now
cto - check this out
cu - see you
cua - see you around
cuitm - see you in the morning
cul - see you later

cul8 - see you later
cuimd - see you in my dreams
cuz - because
cwot - complete waste of time
cwyl - chat with you later
cya - see you
cye - check your e-mail

- D -

da - meaning "The"
dbeyr - don't believe everything you read
dc - disconnect
dcb - dazzling come back
dd - designated driver or due diligence
degt - don't even go there
dga - don't go anywhere
dgaf - don't give a f#%k
dgt - don't go there
dgtg - don't go there, girlfriend
diik - darned if I know
diky - do I know you?
dilligaf - do I look like I give a f#%k?

dis - did I say
diy - do it yourself
dkdc - don't know, don't care
d/l - download
dl - down low
dlbbb - don't let (the) bed bugs bite
dm - doesn't matter
dn - down
dnr - dinner
dnt - don't
dqmot - don't quote me on this
dtf - down to f#%k
dtrt - do the right thing
dts - don't think so
dunno - I don't know
dur - do you remember?
dv8 - deviate
dxnry - dictionary
dykwyatb - do you know what you are talking about?
dyfi - did you find it?
dyor - do your own research

- E -

e1 - everyone

e123 - easy as one, two, three

e2eg - ear to ear grin

ef4t - effort

eg - evil grin

ej - evoking jubilance

em - e-mail

ema - e-mail address

emfbu - excuse me for butting in

enuf - enough

eod - end of discussion or end of day

eol - end of lecture

eol - end of life

eom - end of message

eos - end of show

eot - end of transmission

eta - estimated time (of) arrival

ev - ever

eva - ever

evo - evolution

ez - easy

- F -

f2f - face to face
f2p - free to play
faq - frequently asked questions
fb - feedback or facebook
fbm - fine by me
fbow - for better or worse
fc - fingers crossed
ffa - free for all
ffs - for f#%k's sake
fiik - f#%k if I know
fi - forget it
fil - father in law
fimh - forever in my heart
fitb - fill in the blank
foaf - friend of a friend
fosho - for sure
frt - for real though
ftbomy - from the bottom of my heart
fu - f#%k you
fw - forward

fwiw - for what it's worth
fwm - fine with me
fyeo - for your eyes only
fyi - for your information

- G -

g - great
g2cu - good to see you
g2g - got to go
g2r - got to run
g2ty - got to tell you
g4c - going for coffee
g9 - genius
ga - go ahead
gaas - gentleman and a scholar
gac - get a clue
gal - get a life
gas - got a second?
gb - goodbye
gbtw - get back to work
gd - good
gfi - go for it

gf - girlfriend or good friend
g/f - girlfriend
gg - gotta go
ggoh - gotta get out of here
ggp - gotta go pee
giar - give it a rest
gigo - garbage in, garbage out
gj - good job
gl - good luck
gl2u - good luck to you
gl/hf - good luck, have fun
gmta - great minds think alike
gmv - got my vote
gn - good night
gn/sd - good night, sweet dreams
goi - get over it
gol - giggling out loud
gooh - get out of here
gr8 - great
gratz - congratulations
grl - girl
gt - good try

gtfo - get the f@%k out
gtg - got to go
gtsy - good to see you

- H -

h8tbu - hate to be you
hag1 - have a good one
hau - how about you?
h2cus - hope to see you soon
hagn - have a good night
hago - have a good one
hand - have a nice day
hb - hurry back or happy birthday
hb2u - happy birthday to you
hbday - happy birthday
hbu - how about you?
hf - have fun
hfday - happy father's day
hg - heartfelt guffaw
hmday - happy mother's day
hnh - hot and happenin'
hoas - hold on a second

hth - hope this helps
hv - have
hw - homework

- I -

i2 - I, too (me, too)

ia8 - I already ate

iac - in any case

iae - in any event

iao - I am out (of here)

ib - I'm back

ibiml - I believe in multiple lives

ic - I see

icam - I couldn't agree more

icbw - it could be worse

icedi - I can't even discuss it

icfilwu - I could fall in love with you [see note]

[Note]: You may want to make sure your text recipient is shorthand savvy if you use this one

icymi - in case you missed it

idbi - I don't believe it
idc - I don't care
idgaf - I don't give a f@%k
idk - I don't know
idts - I don't think so
ifyp - I feel your pain
ig2r - I got to run
ig2gp - I got to go pee
ihni - I have no idea
iirc - if I remember correctly
ik - I know
ikr? - I know, right?
lwbl8 - I will be late
ilu - I love you
ily - I love you
imao - in my arrogant opinion
imho - in my honest/humble opinion
imnsho - in my not so humble opinion
imo - in my opinion
ims - I'm sorry
imss - I'm so sorry
isb - I'm so bored

imu - I miss you
io - in/out
iomh - in over my head
iow - in other words
irl - in real life
irmc - I rest my case
islu - I still love you
ituk - I thought you knew
iuss - If you say so
iwalu - I will always love you
iwawo - I want a way out
iykwim - if you know what I mean
iyo - in your opinion
iyss - if you say so

- J -

jam - just a minute
jas - just a second
jff - just for fun
jgi - just google it
jic - just in case
jja - just joking around

jk - just kidding, joking, or joke
jlmk - just let me know
jmo - just my opinion
jp - just playing
jtlyk - just to let you know
jv - joint venture
jw - just wondering

- K -

k - okay
kk - knock knock
kk - okay okay
k/b - keyboard
kb - kick butt
kfy - kiss for you
kia - know it all
kiss - keep it simple, stupid
kit - keep in touch
kma - kiss my @ss
kmb - kiss my butt
koc - kiss on cheek
kol - kiss on lips

kos - kid over shoulder
koso - kind of sort of
kow - knock on wood
kpc - keeping parents clueless
ksc - kind (of) sort (of) chuckle
kutgw - keep up the good work
kwim - know what I mean?
kyhu - keep your head up

- L -

l2g - like/love to go
l2c - like to come
l8 - later
lbay - laughing back at you
ld - later dude, long distance, or low down
ldo - like duh, obviously
lemme - let me
lfd - left for (the) day
lfm - looking for more
lhm - lord help me
lic - like I care

llc - laughing like crazy
lmao - laughing my @ss off
lmbo - laughing my butt off
lmfao - laughing my f#%king ass off
ldi - lets do it
lmirl - let's meet in real life
lmk - let me know
lmno - leave my name out
lnt - lost in translation
loa - list of acronyms
lol - laughing out loud
lolh - laughing out loud hysterically
loti - laughing on the inside
lqtm - laughing quietly to myself
lshmbh - laughing so hard my belly hurts
ltd - living the dream
ltns - long time no see
lts - laughing to self
lu - love you
lult - love you long time
lusm - love you so much
lvm - left voice mail

- M -

m8 - mate

mb - maybe or mamma's boy

mbs - mom behind shoulder

mego - my eyes glaze over

meh - shrugging shoulders, so so, or just alright

mehhh - frustrated shrug

mgmt - management

mirl - meet in real life

mk - mmm okay

mnc - mother nature calls

mo - modus operandi

mod - manager on duty

mof - male or female?

moo - my own opinion

moos - member of opposite sex

mos - mother over shoulder

moss - member of same sex

msg - message

mtf - more to follow

mtfbwu - may the force be with you

mu - miss you
muah - kiss out loud
musm - miss you so much
myo - mind your own
myob - mind your own business

- N -

n1 - nice one
n2m - not too much
nadt - not a damn thing
nalopk - not a lot of people know
nbd - no big deal
nbfab - not bad for a beginner
ne - any
ne1 - anyone
nfh - not for hire
nfm - not for me
nfs - not for sale
nfw - no f#%king way
nfw - not for work
nifoc - naked in front of computer
nigi - now I get it

nimby - not in my back yard
nlt - no later than
nm - never mind
nm - nothing much
nmh - not much here
nmjc - nothing much, just chilling
nmu - not much, you?
nmw - no matter what
nn - not now
no1 - no one
noob - new one on the block or newbie
noyb - none of your business
np - no problem
nrn - no reply necessary
nsa - no strings attached
nt - nice try
nthn - nothing
nts - note to self
nvm - never mind
nvr - never
nw - no way
nwo - no way out

- O -

o4u - only for you

o - hug or oh

oatus - on a totally unrelated subject

ob - oh boy

ob - oh brother

oh - overheard

oic - oh, I see

omdb - over my dead body

omg - oh my God or oh my Goddess

omgug2bk - oh my God, you've got to be kidding

omw - on my way

oo - over and out

ooc - out of character

ooh - out of here

ootd - one of these days

ooto - out of the office

oob - out of bed

op - on phone

orly - oh really?

ot - off topic

otb - off to bed
otfl - on the floor laughing
otl - out to lunch
otoh - on the other hand
otp - on the phone
ott - over the top
ottomh - off the top of my head
otw - off to work
ova - over
oyo - on your own

- P -

p2p - parent to parent
p2p - peer to peer or parent to parent
p911 - parents coming into room, alert
paw - parents are watching
pc - peace or politically correct
pcm - please call me
pda - public display (of) affection
pdh - pretty darn happy
pdsm - please don't shoot me
pdq - pretty darn quick

peeps - people
pfa - pretty f#%king awesome
pft - pretty f#%king tight
pic - picture
pip - peeing in pants (laughing hard)
pir - parents in room
pita - pain in the @ss
pitb - pain in the butt
pl8 - plate
plmk - please let me know
pls - please
plz - please
plztm - please tell me
pm - private Message
pmfi - pardon me for interrupting
pml - pee myself laughing
poahf - put on a happy face
pos - parent over shoulder
pov - point of view
ppl - people
prolly - probably
prt - party

prw - people/parents are watching
psos - parent standing over shoulder
ptiypasi - put that in your pipe and smoke it
ptmm - please tell me more
pu - that stinks!
puk - pick up kids
px - please explain
pyt - pretty young thing
pza - pizza

- Q -

q - question
qfe - question for everyone
qfi - quoted for irony
qik - quick
ql - quit laughing
qq - quick question
qt - cutie
qtpi - cutie pie

- R -

r8 - rate

rbay - right back at you

rfn - right freaking now

rip - rest in peace

rl - real life

rly - really

rme - rolling my eyes

rml - read my lips

rof - rolling on (the) floor

rofl - rolling on floor laughing

roflmfao - rolling on the floor, laughing my freaking ass off

rsn - real soon now

rt - roger that

rtbs - reason to be single

rtrmt - retirement

rtsm - read the stupid manual

ru - are you?

ruk - are you okay?

rut - are you there?

rw - real world

rx - meaning drugs or prescriptions
ryo - roll your own
rys - are you single?

- S -

s2u - same to you
s2s - sorry to say
sat - sorry about that
sb - should be or smiling back
sc - stay cool
sicr - sorry, I couldn't resist
sig2r - sorry, I've got to run
simuc - sorry I missed your call
se2e - smiling ear-to-ear
sfaik - so far as I know
sh - same here
sh^ - shut up
sis - snickering in silence
sit - stay in touch
sk8 - skate
sk8n - skating
sk8r - skater

sk8rb - skater boy
slap - sounds like a plan
smhidb - scratching my head in disbelief
snafu - situation normal all fouled up
snb - shocked and befuddled
snert - snot-nosed, egotistical, rude teenager
so - significant other
soab - son of a b%tch
sol - sooner or later
somy - sick of me yet?
sog - straight or gay?
sos - help!
sot - short on time
sotmg - short on time, must go
sp? - not sure on spelling
spk - speak
srsly - seriously
spst - same place, same time
sq - square
sry - sorry
ss - so sorry

ssdd - same stuff, different day
ssif - so stupid it's funny
ssinf - so stupid it's not funny
st&d - stop texting and drive
stfu - shut the f#%k up
str8 - straight
stw - search the web
sup - what's up?
SUP – stand up paddle
sux - sucks, that sucks
swak - sent with a kiss or sealed with a kiss
swl - screaming with laughter
syl - see you later
sys - see you soon

- T -

t+ - think positively
t2g - time to go
t4bu - thanks for being you
t:)t - think happy thoughts
ta - thanks a lot

tafn - that's all for now

tam - tomorrow a.m.

tau - thinking about you

tbc - to be continued

tbd - to be determined or to be declared

tbh - to be honest

tbhwu - to be honest with you

tbl - text back later

tc - take care

tcob - take care of business

tcoy - take care of yourself

tdtm - talk dirty to me

tff - too freakin' funny

tfs - thanks for sharing

tfti - thanks for the invitation

tg - thank goodness, thank God, or thank Goddess

tgif - thank God(dess) it's Friday

thx - thanks

tht - think happy thoughts

tia - thanks in advance

tiad - tomorrow is another day

tic - tongue-in-cheek
tilii - tell it like it is
tir - teacher in room
ttyl - talk to you later
tl - too long or talk later
tmb - text me back
tmi - too much information
tmot - trust me on this
tmth - too much to handle
tmwfi - take my word for it
tnf - that's not fair
tnstaafl - there's no such thing as a free lunch
tnt - 'til next time
toj - tears of joy
tos - terms of service
tou - thinking of you
tpm - tomorrow p.m.
tptb - the powers that be
tsnf - that's so not fair
tstb - the sooner, the better
tly - totally

tttt - these things take time
ttul - talk to you later
tu - thank you
tusm - thank you so much
twss - that's what she said
ttg - time to go
ttyl - talk to you later
ttys - talk to you soon
ty - thank you
tys - told you so
tyt - take your time
tx - thanks
tysm - thank you so much

- U -

^urs - up yours
ub - unbelievable
ucmu - you crack me up
udi - unidentified drinking injury
ufb - unfreakin' believable
ufn - until further notice
ugtbk - you've got to be kidding

ugtbkm - you've got to be kidding me
ull - you will
una - use no acronyms
uncrtn - uncertain
unpc - un-politically correct
uok? - (are) you ok?
ur - your, you're
ura* - you're a star
urad -you're a dream
urh - you're hot
ursktm - you're so kind to me
urtm - you're the man
urtw – you're the woman
urwlcm - you're welcome
usbca - until something better comes along
usu - usually
ut2l - you take too long
uv - unpleasant visual
uw - you're welcome

- V -

vbs - very big smile
vf - very funny
vgc - very good condition
vip - very important person
vm - voice mail
vn - very nice
vry - very
vsf - very sad face
vwd - very well done

- W -

w - with
w@ - what?
w/b - welcome back
w3- web address
w8 - wait
wah - working at home
waj - what a jerk
wam - wait a minute
wan2 - want to?

wan2t - want to talk
wawa - where are we at?
wayf - where are you from?
wb - write back
wbs - write back soon
wbu - what about you?
wc - welcome
wdalyic - who died and left you in charge
wdyk - what do you know?
wdyt - what do you think?
w/e - whatever
w/end - weekend
wh5 - who, what, when, where, why
wibni - wouldn't it be nice if
wiifm - what's in it for me?
witp - what is the point?
witw - what in the world
wiu - wrap it up
wk - week
wkd - weekend
wrt - with regard to
wo - without

wrk - work
wru@ - where are you at?
wrud - what are you doing?
wtf - what the f#%k?
wibni - wouldn't it be nice if
wtfo - what the F#%k, over!
wtg - way to go
wth - what the heck?
wu - what's up?
wuf - where are you from?
wup - what's up?
wuw - what do you want?
wuu2 - what are you up to?
wwyc - write when you can
wycm - will you call me?
wyd - what are you doing?
wygam - when you get a minute
wyham - when you have a minute
wylei - when you least expect it
wysiwyg - what you see is what you get
wywh - wish you were here

- X -

x - kiss
xL - kiss long and juicy
xme - excuse me
xoxo - hugs & kisses
xlnt - excellent
xyz - examine your zipper

- Y -

y? - why?
y2k - you're too kind
yaa - yet another acronym
ybs - you'll be sorry
ycmu - you crack me up
yf - wife
ygtbkm - you've got to be kidding me
ygg - you go girl
yhbw - you have been warned
yiu - yes, I understand
ykw - you know what
ynk - you never know

yolo - you only live once

yr - year

yt - you there?

ytb - you're the best

yttl - you take too long

ytg - you're the greatest

yw - you're welcome

ywsyls - you win some, you lose some

yyss - yeah yeah sure sure

yyssw - yeah yeah sure sure whatever

- Z -

z - sleepy, boring

za - pizza

zh - sleeping hour

zot - zero tolerance

zup - what's up?

zzz - sleeping, so bored

Language exerts hidden power, like the moon on the tides.

- Rita Mae Brown

Conclusion

So there you have it. You now hold the power to be a better, more efficient communicator via your phone or whatever other device you might choose to use. Go and have fun with it! Yes, having fun is perfectly acceptable and even highly encouraged.

Enjoy, be well, and take pride in your texting, but, like when doing anything else, not too much pride. ;)

Notes

About the Author

Justin Bilancieri is a creative living in Boulder, Colorado. This is his first published book. He's produced a documentary called *Sustainable America*, which can be viewed at www.awarepictures.com. He is an avid outdoorsman, musician, plant-based eater, and has a passion for making the world a better place. Keep tabs on him or give him a shout at www.JustinBilancieri.com.

Made in the USA
Columbia, SC
22 August 2019